Original title:
Picking Up Pieces

Copyright © 2024 Swan Charm
All rights reserved.

Author: Daisy Dewi
ISBN HARDBACK: 978-9916-79-218-6
ISBN PAPERBACK: 978-9916-79-219-3
ISBN EBOOK: 978-9916-79-220-9

The Blessing of Imperfection

In shadows cast by fleeting grace,
We find the light in every place.
With cracks that hum a sacred song,
In brokenness, we all belong.

Each flaw a spark, each scar a sign,
In tangled vines our spirits twine.
The beauty lies in what is real,
A tapestry of hearts that heal.

In whispered prayers, we come anew,
Embracing doubts, our faith shines through.
Through trials faced, our souls align,
In imperfections, love will shine.

The warmth of grace in every tear,
A journey shared, both far and near.
In every stumble, hope will rise,
For in our flaws, the spirit flies.

So let us walk with gentle pride,
With open hearts, we'll turn the tide.
The blessing found in every part,
In imperfectness, we'll find our heart.

The Anthem of Assembled Hearts

Together we rise, in truth we stand,
Linked by faith, hand in hand.
An anthem sweet, a sacred call,
In unity, we shall not fall.

With each word sung, a bond so tight,
In love's embrace, we find the light.
Voices joined, a melody pure,
In every heart, our souls endure.

Through stormy skies and blazing suns,
Each burden shared, our healing runs.
In laughter, tears, we find our way,
Assembled hearts shall never sway.

In sacred space, where spirits soar,
Together we seek, forevermore.
With every note, let joy impart,
The anthem lives within our heart.

So let us sing, let praises rise,
In harmony, our spirits prize.
For the world is bright, as we uphold,
The anthem of love, a story told.

Candlelight in the Chaos

In darkness thick, a flicker glows,
A humble flame where hope now flows.
Amidst the storm, a quiet plea,
For peace to reign, for hearts to see.

With every breath, we seek the light,
In chaos fierce, faith takes its flight.
Candle's warmth, a beacon bright,
Guiding souls through endless night.

So gather close, hold hands in prayer,
For in His love, we find our air.
Together bound, we share our grace,
In candlelight, we find our place.

The Alchemy of Grace

From ashes rise, a heart reborn,
In trials faced, the spirit's worn.
Transmuted gold from burdens deep,
In grace, restored, we learn to leap.

With every tear, a lesson learned,
In fire's forge, our souls are turned.
The breaking point, a sacred start,
Where fractured pieces form the heart.

The alchemy of love divine,
Transforms our pain, our hearts align.
In gratitude, we lift our voice,
For in His arms, we find our choice.

Gathered Souls of Silence

In quietude, our spirits dwell,
In hushed embrace, we share our shell.
Gathered round the sacred ground,
In silent prayer, our truths are found.

The stillness speaks in whispers low,
A gentle guide through ebb and flow.
Hearts intertwined in sacred trust,
From shadowed depths, we rise, we must.

Together forged in love's embrace,
In silence deep, we find our grace.
Each soul a candle, brightly burned,
In gathered light, our spirits turned.

Words from the Wounded

From aching hearts, the truth does flow,
In darkest nights, the pain does grow.
Yet through the wounds, a story speaks,
A path of strength that hope bespeaks.

Each scar a mark of battles fought,
Lessons learned, and wisdom sought.
In trials faced, we rise again,
For every fall, we shall ascend.

Words from the wounded, healing sounds,
In every heart, compassion bounds.
Together we share our fragile grace,
In love's embrace, we find our place.

Pillars of Strength

In faith we stand through the storm,
Each prayer a shield to keep us warm.
With hearts united, we rise anew,
Guided by light that shines so true.

From trials faced, we've gained our might,
In darkest hours, we seek the light.
Love binds our spirits, a sacred thread,
In every tear, a truth is said.

Mountains tremble, yet we remain,
Our souls uplifted, free from pain.
With every challenge, we grow bold,
In the arms of grace, our hearts turned gold.

Voices raised in harmonious praise,
We find our courage in endless days.
Together we build on these strong beams,
A sanctuary woven from our dreams.

Through kindness shared, we heal the rift,
In gentle whispers, our spirits lift.
The pillars stand, unshaken, strong,
In unity found, we all belong.

Devotion in Disarray

In shadows deep, our spirits wane,
Lost in twists of heart's refrain.
Yet still we search for paths to light,
Hope flickers soft in darkest night.

With whispered prayers that drift like smoke,
In scattered dreams, we slowly choke.
Yet faith ignites a spark so small,
Through tangled threads, we hear the call.

Each shattered trust, a lesson learned,
In chaos' grip, our hearts have yearned.
Through torn pages, we find our way,
In fractured hope, new dawns will play.

Amidst the noise, a quiet grace,
Binds us together in this space.
Through every struggle, we stand tall,
In devotion's dance, we rise and fall.

Through cracks and flaws, love finds its way,
Restoring hope in the light of day.
In disarray, the heart can mend,
Together in faith, our spirits blend.

The Hopeful Canvas

A canvas blank, awaits our dreams,
Each brushstroke speaks in sacred themes.
Colors blend in a gentle dance,
Expressing hearts in a timeless trance.

With every shade, our stories told,
In vibrant hues, both brave and bold.
Faith paints the skies in endless grace,
A masterpiece in every place.

From darkened shades, the light breaks through,
In strokes of hope, our spirits grew.
Unseen hands guide the seeker's plight,
Transforming darkness into light.

Each layer tells of pain and joy,
In holy art, we see the ploy.
Together, we craft the tale of life,
In unity found amidst the strife.

The canvas wide, with endless space,
Invites us all to seek our place.
In colors shared, we find our peace,
Through strokes of love, our doubts and cease.

Wings of the Repaired

From broken dreams, new wings arise,
Restored in faith, we touch the skies.
With every scar, a story glows,
In gentle winds, our spirit flows.

Frayed edges tell of battles won,
In trials faced, we see the sun.
Each whispered prayer a soft caress,
Through whispered winds, we find our rest.

Through stormy nights and weary days,
We search for strength in love's embrace.
In every struggle, the heart finds cheer,
As faith unveils all that we hold dear.

Together we rise, no need to fear,
With open hearts, we draw you near.
The wings we sport, once broken, bare,
Now soar the heavens, light as air.

In unity, our voices soar,
With wings repaired, we seek once more.
Through love restored, we find our way,
In hope reborn with each new day.

Renewal Beneath the Fractured Sky

In shadows deep where silence flows,
The heart's lament, a river knows.
Yet whispers rise, a tender call,
Hope's gentle touch, it breaks the fall.

Beneath the sky, both cracked and wide,
A promise glows, a faith inside.
The earth remembers, the spirit sings,
In every sorrow, renewal springs.

From broken clay, new vessels form,
Embracing love, a sacred norm.
Together we weave, a tapestry bright,
In sacred spaces, we find the light.

So lift your gaze, when darkness looms,
For in the night, fresh hope blooms.
With every breath, let gratitude rise,
Renewal waits beneath the skies.

Grace After the Collapse

In crumbled dreams, the spirit grieves,
Yet in the ash, a promise weaves.
Through shattered stones, a whisper glows,
Grace flows freely, as love bestows.

From tangled roots, new life will spark,
In desolation, still there's a mark.
The strength of faith, a guiding star,
Lifts weary souls, no matter how far.

When hope seems lost, and shadows creep,
In sacred trust, we find our keep.
The dust may settle, the night may fall,
Yet grace surrounds, embracing all.

With open hearts, let healing flow,
In every loss, true love will grow.
From ashes rise, our voices blend,
In unity, we find our mend.

The Light After the Fall

When darkness swathes the weary heart,
In yet another day we start.
The dawn, a beacon, breaks the night,
A gentle touch, a sacred light.

In every stumble, in every tear,
The spirit whispers, 'Do not fear.'
For after storms, the sun will reign,
In trials faced, our strength is gained.

From heights we've tumbled into grace,
In fractured soil, a holy space.
With every breath, we rise anew,
In love's embrace, our visions true.

So trust the path, though steep it seems,
For light will follow your deepest dreams.
In every fall, we learn to stand,
United in hope, hand in hand.

Remnants of the Beloved

In sacred whispers, love persists,
Amidst the chaos, hope exists.
The remnants of the beloved flow,
In every heart, their essence glows.

With jasmine scents and morning light,
They cradle souls through darkest night.
In laughter shared and tears released,
The bonds of love will never cease.

Memories woven, a gentle thread,
In quiet moments where souls tread.
Though bodies fade, their spirits soar,
In every heartbeat, they are more.

Let love remain, a timeless hymn,
In every loss, our hearts will brim.
For in the echo of their grace,
We find a way, we find our place.

The Resurrection of Joy

From shadows deep, a light will shine,
Hearts once heavy, now entwined.
In the stillness, a voice does call,
Rise in hope, do not fall.

Grace like rivers freely flows,
In each echo, the Spirit glows.
Awake, arise, let praises sing,
Joy reborn, our offering.

The dawn breaks forth, a promise near,
Faith ignites, dispelling fear.
In laughter's dance, we stand embraced,
In this journey, love is traced.

Mountains tremble, seas rejoice,
In the silence, we hear His voice.
Each tear cried, a seed to sow,
From pain's ashes, new life grows.

With open hearts, we gather here,
Together, erasing every fear.
In joy's embrace, we find the way,
To celebrate this new-found day.

Bounty from Burnt Offerings

Come forth, O grain, from fertile earth,
An act of love, a sacred birth.
With fire's kiss, our gifts we raise,
In humble service, we bring our praise.

The altar waits, a sacred space,
Each offering, a sign of grace.
In smoke that rises, prayers ascend,
In this moment, hearts will mend.

With every harvest, blessings flow,
In steadfast faith, our spirits grow.
From sacrifice, we learn to yield,
In gratitude, our souls are healed.

Let gratitude be our constant prayer,
In giving, we find love to share.
As flames do dance, our souls ignite,
In unity, we embrace the light.

From burnt offerings, hope is born,
A tapestry of love, well-worn.
In this bounty, let us unite,
To honor Him, our guiding light.

A Symphony of Forgiveness

In gentle whispers, peace descends,
A melody that never ends.
With open hearts, we seek to mend,
In every wound, a chance to blend.

Forgive the past, release the chains,
In love's embrace, true freedom reigns.
Together we rise, hand in hand,
In harmony, a sacred band.

Compassion flows like rivers wide,
In every tear, a love implied.
Each note we play, a heart's refrain,
In grace, we learn to live again.

With every step, we find our way,
In unity, we brightly stay.
A symphony, in every soul,
Forgiveness deepens, makes us whole.

Through trials faced, we sing in rhyme,
In love's embrace, redeeming time.
Our song of hope, a sacred gift,
In every heart, our spirits lift.

Unbroken Fellowship

In every gathering, Spirit flows,
A bond unbroken, love bestows.
Hearts entwined, in joy we stand,
Together, we journey hand in hand.

In laughter shared, in sorrows too,
A fellowship that's pure and true.
With open arms, we greet the day,
In kindness found, we light the way.

Through trials faced and battles fought,
In love's embrace, all lessons taught.
Together we rise, together we fall,
In every moment, we heed His call.

With every prayer, our spirits soar,
In shared grace, we seek for more.
In unbroken friendship, we aspire,
To share the warmth of heaven's fire.

As seasons change and time moves on,
In unity, our hearts are drawn.
In fellowship, life's puzzle fit,
In every love, His grace be lit.

Gifts from the Shattered

In broken vessels, light shines bright,
From pain and sorrow, emerges right.
Fractured dreams, yet hope does bloom,
From shattered hearts, the Spirit's room.

Each crack and tear tells a tale,
Of grace that flows like a gentle gale.
In darkness birthed, the dawn will rise,
True strength is found when we empathize.

Wisdom found in weary souls,
Embraced by Him, our lives made whole.
In every loss, a treasure's gleam,
In shattered dreams, we find our theme.

So gather the pieces, let hearts unite,
In flawed perfection, we see His light.
The gifts we carry, though bruised and worn,
Emit a beauty, though tattered and torn.

For in the ruins, purpose lies,
From shattered paths, we learn to rise.
These gifts are seeds of hope, we sow,
In every crack, let love still flow.

Holy Threads Weaved

In sacred looms, our lives entwined,
With threads of love, the heart designed.
Each fiber woven, unique and pure,
In holy patterns, we find our cure.

Through trials faced, the threads grow tight,
In unity's warmth, we find more light.
A tapestry rich with wisdom's thread,
In every stitch, His love is spread.

Fates interlaced, and spirits soar,
Through woven paths, we seek the lore.
Each part connected, a divine embrace,
In the fabric of faith, we find our place.

So let us cherish each thread entwined,
For in our stories, His love aligned.
In every struggle, the weaver's grace,
Holds together the human race.

Together we rise, as garments share,
In holy threads, we find our prayer.
Bound by love, no heart will fray,
In sacred weavings, we praise each day.

Seraphic Scars

In holy wounds, beauty appears,
Each seraphic scar tells of years.
Through trials borne and battles fought,
In every mark, a lesson taught.

In fragile flesh, a story lies,
Of faith's endurance, and angel's cries.
This sacred hurt, a path to grace,
In scars, we see His warm embrace.

With tender hands, He holds each seam,
In brokenness, we find the dream.
The light shines through the shattered parts,
In every scar, He mends our hearts.

These seraphic scars, our honor wear,
A testament of love and care.
In memories forged, our strength is gleaned,
In every wound, His promise gleaned.

So let us walk with scars displayed,
In every journey, unafraid.
For through our wounds, His glory streams,
In seraphic scars, He plants our dreams.

Vessels of Grace

We are but vessels, cracked and true,
Filled with grace, in all we do.
In fertile soil, we sow His love,
Anointed spirits, guided from above.

With each outpouring, we share the light,
Transforming darkness, turning plight.
In humble hearts, His presence flows,
Through every challenge, the river grows.

Each life a story, rich and deep,
In shadows cast, the promise we keep.
As vessels filled, we share our fate,
In service rendered, we elevate.

For in our capacity, hope we find,
To heal the broken, gentle and kind.
With every giving, we minister grace,
In love's embrace, we find our space.

So let us be vessels, open wide,
Pouring out love, with Him as guide.
For every moment, we stand in place,
Reflecting His light, as vessels of grace.

Restoration of the Heart's Light

In shadows deep, where spirits weep,
The softest whisper calls us near.
With gentle hands, He mends the break,
And in His grace, we find our cheer.

A flicker glows beneath the ash,
As love's warm embrace brings us home.
United souls, we rise and soar,
Transforming dust, we freely roam.

For every wound, a testament,
Of carried burdens, love unseen.
In brokenness, we find the way,
To shine anew, our hearts serene.

Let not despair eclipse the dawn,
In faith, our spirits find their flight.
Through trials faced, our hearts ignite,
Restoring what was lost to night.

Gathering the Lost Offerings

In fields of doubt, we seek the lost,
Each weary soul, a jewel bright.
With open arms, we gather close,
To share in love's redemptive light.

The whispered prayers, like morning dew,
Refresh the weary, heart by heart.
In sacrament of sacred grace,
We learn that every soul's a part.

With each compassion, offerings rise,
As fragrant smoke towards the sky.
In unity, our hearts align,
To lift the broken, to reply.

Embracing shadows, we find peace,
Each lost and broken now restored.
Through tender bonds, we make a place,
Where love's pure echo is adored.

The Alchemy of Brokenness

In shattered souls, we find the gold,
The beauty born from deep despair.
Like phoenix flames that rise from dust,
A miracle awaits us there.

Each scar a story, rich and true,
A tapestry of love and pain.
In fractured hearts, creation blooms,
From every loss, our hope we gain.

With courage, we can face the night,
Transforming pain to radiant light.
Inventing joy from sorrow's grasp,
In brokenness, all things unite.

So lift your eyes and see the art,
The alchemy within the tears.
In the depths of our shared plight,
We cultivate our faith through fears.

Faith in the Fragments

In pieces scattered far and wide,
We gather what remains, our trust.
With heartbeats echoing the truth,
In fragments, lies the sacred dust.

For every doubt that clouds our sight,
Faith whispers softly, 'Do not fear.'
In every crack, a glimpse of light,
Revealing grace is ever near.

The tapestry of hope we weave,
From threads of sorrow, joy will spring.
United in this noble quest,
Our voices rise to praise and sing.

Embrace the fractured, hold it close,
Each broken part sings praise anew.
In faith's embrace, the heart shall soar,
Transformed by love, forever true.

Eclipsed Blessings

In shadows cast by the light,
We seek the grace of the night.
Each trial brings forth a spark,
Guiding us through the dark.

Cherished gifts cloaked in pain,
A faith that rises again.
In loss, we find our gain,
The sun will shine after rain.

Whispers of hope from above,
Infusing our hearts with love.
In silence, the spirit sings,
Revealing the joy that it brings.

Eclipsed yet shining so bright,
Transforming despair into light.
Through valleys of sorrow we tread,
A path where the faithful are led.

Trust in the journey divine,
For blessings are not hard to find.
In every tear, in every sigh,
God's promise will never die.

Embracing the Splinters

In the wood where hearts may break,
The pieces of us we must take.
For every splinter holds a story,
A testament wrapped in glory.

Through pain, we learn to be whole,
A whispering truth in our soul.
These shards, though sharp, they remind,
Divine love often entwined.

Holding fast to the bruised divine,
In each fracture, a love will shine.
Wounds healed by hands so kind,
In brokenness, hope is defined.

Embrace the scars of the past,
In grace and mercy, we're cast.
From the splinters, strength will rise,
Renewed vision through the skies.

Through the trials we dare to face,
We find our truest embrace.
In every crack, every seam,
Lies the truth of a sacred dream.

Cradle of Restoration

In the quiet of the night,
A promise glows, soft and bright.
The cradle of life, tender and warm,
Brings peace amidst every storm.

From ashes, we rise anew,
Each breath reveals a clearer view.
In the stillness, hope is found,
As love gathers all around.

With hands that mend and heal,
The heart's wounds begin to seal.
Divine whispers guide the way,
Transforming night into day.

In every tear that we've shed,
Is a seed of love that's been fed.
For in restoration's embrace,
We discover our rightful place.

Let faith be the light we follow,
Through shadows deep and hollow.
In each dawn, a fresh start,

The cradle of grace holds our heart.

The Harvest of Hardship

In fields that bloom with strife,
We cultivate the strength of life.
Through trials that seem unfair,
Planting seeds of love and care.

Resilience grows in rough terrain,
Nurtured by the drops of rain.
In every struggle, we find our way,
A harvest crafted from dismay.

With each obstacle, we learn to bend,
Knowing hardships can be a friend.
In labor, there lies a gift,
As our weary spirits lift.

Gathering wisdom from the pain,
In heart's embrace, we break the chain.
For every shadow has its streak,
Of light that graces, soft and meek.

The harvest yields a fragrant bloom,
From every heartache, blessings loom.
In faith, we find our truest gain,
From hardship's soil, love shall reign.

The Testament of Trials

In shadows deep, where faith is tried,
The spirit weeps, yet will abide.
A whisper calls through darkest night,
In trials faced, we find the light.

Each sorrow bears a sacred sign,
In broken hearts, the grace will shine.
Through storms we walk, with heads held high,
A testament, our souls will fly.

The path is steep, yet love will guide,
With every step, we turn the tide.
In moments fraught, we rise anew,
For in our trials, grace breaks through.

The winds may howl, the earth may quake,
Yet in our trust, we will not break.
With hands held fast, our spirits soar,
The testament, forevermore.

Through tears we learn, through pain we grow,
In sacred bonds, our hearts aglow.
This journey shared, in faith we roam,
In every trial, we find our home.

Beacons of Restoration

In quiet dawn, the light appears,
A beacon bright, to calm our fears.
With open hearts, we seek the way,
Restoration blooms with each new day.

From ashes rise, the soul renewed,
In humble grace, our paths pursued.
Through darkest night, the stars will shine,
In every heart, the truth divine.

Embrace the light, let shadows fade,
With every step, our hope displayed.
The ties of love, forever strong,
In unity, we all belong.

With hands outstretched, we mend our ties,
In every soul, a spark that flies.
Together, we ignite the flame,
Beacons bright, we share one name.

In harmony, our voices blend,
A symphony that will not end.
Through trials faced, our hearts will sing,
Restoration found in everything.

The Seal of Renewal

A sacred bond, a silent vow,
In whispered prayers, we meet the now.
With every breath, we seek the true,
The seal of renewal, born anew.

In Nature's hands, we find our place,
In every trial, a touch of grace.
The past released, we chase the dawn,
With open hearts, our fears are gone.

Through storms of doubt, we journey forth,
Each moment shines, revealing worth.
In every tear, a lesson learned,
The flame of hope, forever burned.

The path of love, a winding road,
In every heart, our spirits flowed.
A seal of promise, pure and bright,
In unity, we find our light.

With faith as guide, we rise above,
A testament to endless love.
In grace we stand, our spirits soar,
Renewed in heart, forevermore.

Hearts Reclaimed

In quiet spaces, hearts once lost,
Are gently found, no greater cost.
With every tear that stains the ground,
A story shared, our souls unbound.

Through trials faced, we learn to see,
In brokenness, our unity.
Embrace the scars, they tell our tale,
In every heart, love will prevail.

With open arms, we welcome grace,
A journey shared, a sacred space.
In laughter's joy, in sorrow's pain,
Together still, our hearts reclaimed.

In every moment, hand in hand,
We forge the ties that ever stand.
Beyond the storms that life unfolds,
Our hearts reclaimed, the truth it holds.

So let us walk this path as one,
In dusk's embrace, the rising sun.
With every heartbeat, love will reign,
In unity, our hearts reclaimed.

Shattered Hopes

In silence, dreams collapse and fade,
A whispered prayer for light unmade.
With every tear, a promise lost,
Yet faith remains, despite the cost.

The shadows linger, doubts arise,
Yet still I seek the distant skies.
For in the heart, hope must reside,
An ember glows, it must not hide.

Through valleys deep, the path is rough,
Yet in the struggle, we find the tough.
Each fracture tells a story bold,
Of battles fought, and truths retold.

When night is long, and spirits low,
A gentle hand begins to show.
The shards of dreams may pierce the soul,
Yet God will gather, make us whole.

Awake, arise, and take the stand,
In shattered hopes, He holds our hand.
For through the pain, a new song plays,
In brokenness, our faith's rebays.

Reclaimed Faith

A lighthouse stands on stormy sea,
Its beam a guide for you and me.
In darkest hours, we seek the shore,
A call to hope, forevermore.

When shadows dim and fears take flight,
His loving grace restores the light.
From ashes rise, the spirit strong,
In reclaimed faith, we find our song.

Each step unveiled, a journey wide,
With every trial, He stands beside.
Through valleys deep and mountains high,
In faith we soar, like wings to fly.

In quiet moments, whispers come,
Promises made, we're never numb.
In every heart, a spark ignites,
Reclaimed faith shines, like countless lights.

Together we advance as one,
No longer lost, but brightly spun.
For in His arms, we find our way,
With reclaimed faith, we greet the day.

Fragments of Grace

In every tear, a gift bestowed,
A tapestry from love's abode.
Each fragment shines, though worn and torn,
In grace we rise, anew reborn.

The world may break, the heart may strain,
Yet in the storm, we find no pain.
For grace abides, a tender cloak,
In every word, His love invoked.

As dawn approaches, light breaks free,
In fragments, glimpses of destiny.
Together bound, our spirits soar,
With grace, we walk through every door.

In brokenness, His kindness flows,
A river wide, where mercy grows.
Each moment shared, a treasure rare,
In fragments of grace, we find His care.

So take my hand, we'll journey far,
With fragments bright, like shining stars.
In every heart, His love's embrace,
Together in these fragments of grace.

Mend the Broken Vessel

A vessel cracked, its beauty marred,
Yet still it holds a soul, unmarred.
With gentle hands, He starts to weave,
The art of love, we must believe.

In every crack, a story lies,
Of battles fought and gentle sighs.
He fills the gaps with warmth so bright,
A mended heart, restored to light.

Though scars may linger, hope remains,
Through trials faced, and wounds that pains.
For in the Lord's embrace, we stand,
He molds the clay with guiding hand.

In whispered prayers, the healing starts,
A symphony, the mended hearts.
With every breath, we rise and sing,
The beauty found in every spring.

Together, hand in hand we tread,
A journey blessed, where angels tread.
Mend the vessel, let love flow,
In brokenness, His strength will show.

Sanctuary of Scattered Souls

In quiet corners, hearts aligned,
A sanctuary where love's defined.
In scattered souls, we find our place,
United strong in endless grace.

Each tear that falls, a sacred bond,
In every story, we respond.
Together, we rise through trials vast,
In harmony, we forge our past.

The broken paths, the winding ways,
Lead us to brighter, hopeful days.
Each whispered prayer, a bridge to Him,
In scattered souls, our fears grow dim.

With open hearts, we seek to heal,
In every wound, His love can seal.
In solitude, we won't remain,
For in His arms, we shed the pain.

Together, let our voices rise,
A sanctuary beneath the skies.
In scattered souls, we find the whole,
In love divine, we heal the soul.

Echoes of the Divine Heart

In silence, I hear the whispers glow,
A melody soft, like a river's flow.
Each beat of the heart, a sacred call,
Guiding our souls, lest we stumble and fall.

In shadows of doubt, faith takes its flight,
Illuminating paths when all seems night.
With hands raised high, we seek the embrace,
Of grace that surrounds us, a warm, gentle place.

The echoes of love in each quiet prayer,
Binding the spirits, lifting despair.
Together we rise, in spirit, we mend,
For whispers divine are the notes that transcends.

In community's cradle, we find our peace,
Shared burdens diminish, our troubles cease.
A symphony strong, united we stand,
Echoes of the heart reach across every land.

Pilgrimage Through Shattered Dreams

We walk the path marked by tears and pain,
Each step a struggle, a heavy chain.
Yet through the darkness, a flicker of light,
A promise of hope in the long, weary night.

The dreams we held tight now lie in the dust,
But faith breathes life, in God we trust.
With every heartbreak, a lesson remains,
Finding the beauty in fragile refrains.

As pilgrims we gather, with stories to share,
What once was broken, now finds repair.
Through valleys of despair, we journey on,
For dawn follows night, and hope is reborn.

With courage, we rise, hand in hand we tread,
From shattered illusions, new dreams are bred.
In the quiet moments, our spirits entwined,
We discover the strength that love has aligned.

The road may be long, yet together we go,
Held by a vision that thrives in the flow.
Pilgrims of light, we search and we seek,
For within every fracture, the soul learns to speak.

From Desolation to Devotion

In barren fields where no blooms appear,
A heart once heavy now dares to steer.
From ashes to hope, through trials we rise,
With faith as our compass, towards endless skies.

Each tear that has fallen a seed in the ground,
Watered by love, our spirits unbound.
In the garden of grace, we tend to our souls,
Transforming the silence, as harmony rolls.

From desolation's grasp, we learn to rebirth,
Discovering purpose, our infinite worth.
In shadows of doubt, devotion ignites,
Lighting the path with divine, holy lights.

With every small gesture, love's echoes expand,
Bridge gaps of the heart with a gentle hand.
From the depths of sorrow, we rise and we sing,
In the chapters of faith, our voices take wing.

So let us be vessels for light to flow free,
Bound together by love, eternally.
For from desolation, devotion takes flight,
Embracing the dawn, a glorious sight.

Rebuilding the Temple of the Soul

From crumbled ruins, we gather the stone,
With hands intertwined, never alone.
Each piece a story, each crack, a sign,
Of battles endured, and souls that align.

With patience and care, we raise up the walls,
A temple of love, where the spirit calls.
Echoes of laughter, the sound of a prayer,
A sanctuary built on the strength that we share.

In the quiet spaces where shadows once lay,
New light emerges, turning night into day.
Through trials and triumph, the heart must refine,
Rebuilding with purpose, in sacred design.

Together we stand, with a vision so clear,
Through each act of kindness, we draw ever near.
The temple we build is a masterpiece true,
A refuge of faith, where all can renew.

So let us be builders, with love as our guide,
In the architecture of faith, let's abide.
For as we rise up, the soul finds its role,
Rebuilding together the temple of soul.

Cupped Hands of Refuge

In the quiet of night we seek,
With cupped hands, our hearts speak.
A shelter of grace from above,
Holding secrets of endless love.

The storms may rage, the winds may blow,
But safe in His arms, we always know.
The light will guide our weary way,
In His refuge, we forever stay.

With every breath, we find our peace,
In prayer, our burdens slowly cease.
Cupped hands raised, we share our plea,
In His embrace, we are truly free.

Together we rise, united in prayer,
Finding comfort in the love we share.
In whispers of hope, we find our tune,
Cupped hands of refuge beneath the moon.

Through trials faced, we're never alone,
In His presence, we've all grown.
With faith as our shield, and love as our guide,
Cupped hands of refuge, forever abide.

Cracked but Glorious

In brokenness, we find the light,
Cracked but glorious, souls take flight.
Fragmented hearts, still they sing,
Of hope and grace, a radiant spring.

Through trials faced, we still believe,
In every crack, love weaves reprieve.
The beauty lies in scars we bear,
Each marked line a whispered prayer.

In shadows cast, we rise anew,
Cracked but glorious, shining through.
Each wound a tale, each tear a song,
In the arms of grace, we all belong.

The potter shapes, with hands so kind,
Embracing flaws with love intertwined.
Cracked but glorious, we find our worth,
In our brokenness, we claim rebirth.

With every heartbeat, we choose to shine,
In the tapestry, His love divine.
Cracked but glorious, we stand in pride,
In the arms of grace, we abide.

The Path of Forgiveness

On the trail where mercy flows,
The path of forgiveness softly grows.
Each step we take, a choice we make,
To shed the burdens, for love's sake.

In shadows cast by anger's reign,
We find the strength to break the chain.
With open hearts, we set a course,
For healing grace, a gentle force.

As we release the grief and pain,
The burdens light, like falling rain.
Each act of love, a fragrant gift,
On the path of forgiveness, spirits lift.

With whispered prayers, we seek to mend,
In humble hearts, we find a friend.
The path unravels, with hope and light,
Forgiveness blooms in the quiet night.

Together we walk, hand in hand,
A journey sweet, on sacred land.
In the grace of love, we rise above,
The path of forgiveness leads to love.

Shards in the Sunlight

In the morning light, they gleam and glow,
Shards in the sunlight, tales to bestow.
Each piece a story, scattered and bright,
Reflecting hope in the purest light.

Wounded fragments that once felt lost,
Now sparkle proudly, no matter the cost.
Gathering strength from the trials faced,
Shards in the sunlight, perfectly placed.

Through storms of doubt, we push and strive,
In every shard, the heart's alive.
Colors of grace, they rise and sing,
In the warmth of love, new life we bring.

As shadows dance in the fading night,
Shards in the sunlight, revealing light.
Embracing the flaws that once brought pain,
In each little piece, our faith remains.

Together we shine, in unity bound,
In every shimmer, His love is found.
Shards in the sunlight, a miraculous art,
Reflecting the beauty of the broken heart.

Wings of Ascent

In quiet prayer, our spirits lift,
A heavenly breeze, a sacred gift.
With faith, we soar, on wings of light,
Guided by love, through darkest night.

Through trials faced, our hearts remain,
In joy and sorrow, our souls sustain.
Each step we take, in grace we've found,
The path is true, where hope abounds.

The light above, it calls us near,
With every whisper, we lose our fear.
In unity, we rise as one,
To seek the warmth of the shining sun.

May kindness flow, like rivers wide,
In every heart, let love abide.
Our spirits bright, we claim the day,
With every breath, we'll find our way.

As wings unfold, we take our flight,
To realms of peace, in purest light.
Together bound, we lift our voice,
In love we trust, in hope rejoice.

Grace in the Aftermath

When shadows fall and silence lingers,
In brokenness, we find our fingers.
To piece together what was torn,
In grace, we rise, again reborn.

The storm may rage, the winds may howl,
Yet through the night, we hear love's prowl.
In every tear, a lesson learned,
In ashes cold, our spirits burned.

With open hands, we seek the light,
Through every struggle, we gain our sight.
The road ahead may twist and bend,
But in His arms, we find our friend.

We walk this path, though bruised and scarred,
With each small step, our souls are marred.
Yet beauty blooms where hearts align,
In every crack, the light will shine.

The aftermath, a canvas bare,
We paint with love, beyond despair.
In every moment, grace will flow,
Through trials faced, our spirits grow.

The Blessing of the Frayed

In threads of life, we weave our tale,
Each moment lived, a fragile sail.
With every tear, a story spun,
In frayed moments, we are one.

When burdens weigh, the heart may bend,
Yet in our fall, there's strength to mend.
A tapestry of joy and pain,
In unity, we rise again.

The blessing found in trials small,
Each whispered prayer, we heed the call.
Through tangled paths, our spirits seek,
In humble hearts, we find the meek.

The frayed edges, they hold the gold,
In every heart, a story told.
We gather close, hand in hand,
In faith we stand, like grains of sand.

Together bound, we sew the seams,
In shared vision, we chase our dreams.
The blessing of the frayed we claim,
In love's embrace, we find our flame.

Risen from the Dust

From humble ground, our roots entwine,
In every heartbeat, divinity's sign.
With dreams awakened, we find our rise,
In life's embrace, the spirit flies.

Each stumble made, a step to grace,
In shadows cast, we seek His face.
Through trials faced, our hearts hold fast,
In every moment, the die is cast.

The dust we tread, a sacred ground,
In whispers soft, His love is found.
With every dawn, our hope reborn,
In love's embrace, we are adorned.

We rise as one, from depths so low,
In every heart, a fire will grow.
The past may haunt, but forward we tread,
With courage strong, the light ahead.

Risen from the dust, we stand in grace,
With open hands, we seek His face.
In every trial, our spirits trust,
Together we rise, from the dust.

The Ark of New Beginnings

In waters deep, a vessel sails,
Carved by faith, where hope prevails.
A promise made, a covenant sealed,
In the storm's eye, His love revealed.

With every dawn, a chance is born,
To rise anew, from trials worn.
The rainbows arch, the skies declare,
That every heart can find repair.

From ashes rise, through pain and strife,
In hands of grace, we find our life.
The ark it floats on sacred tides,
In faith and truth, the spirit guides.

As creatures join in harmony,
A testament of unity.
Together strong, through waves we'll glide,
In His embrace, we shall abide.

Believe, dear soul, this journey vast,
For in His arms, we stand steadfast.
The ark of hope forever sails,
In love divine, our spirit prevails.

Embracing the Fragments

In shattered dreams, His light will stream,
Each broken piece, a sacred theme.
Embrace the scars, let healing start,
For wholeness blooms within the heart.

The tapestry of life unfolds,
In threads of love, the mystery molds.
With every tear, a story weaves,
In gentle grace, the spirit frees.

Together bound, in joy and pain,
The sun must shine to bless the rain.
These fragments hold the truth we seek,
In joyful whispers, the spirit speaks.

So gather close, each shard divine,
In collective song, our souls align.
Around the fire of grace we stand,
In unity, we bless this land.

Embrace the fragments, let them show,
In love's reflection, how we grow.
For in the cracks, He lights the way,
In brokenness, we find our play.

Lament and Light

In shadows cast, the heart does weep,
For all we've lost, and what we keep.
The echoes ring of trials faced,
Yet in the dark, His hope is traced.

Lament we sing, with souls laid bare,
In honest tears, we find our prayer.
Each sorrow shared, a sacred thread,
A bridge to light, where angels tread.

Through valleys low, we journey still,
His whispered strength, our aching will.
In every cry, a promise near,
That dawn will break, and bring us cheer.

Lift up your eyes, the stars will shine,
In every wound, His love aligns.
Together forged in grief and grace,
We rise anew, in His embrace.

So let us sing, through pain and strife,
In lament deep, we find our life.
And through the night, the light will rise,
In every tear, the soul complies.

The Resurrection Palette

From muted hues, the dawn awakes,
With colors bright, the canvas shakes.
Each stroke of faith, a vibrant scene,
In shadows cast, the light is seen.

With every shade, we feel the grace,
In trials faced, our hearts embrace.
The palette wide, with love it flows,
A masterpiece that only grows.

Rebirth unfolds in golden light,
As hopes arise to take their flight.
In spirit's dance, we find our way,
To paint new dreams in bright array.

Together joined, our colors blend,
In unity, we shall transcend.
For resurrection sings so sweet,
In every heart, where love's complete.

So brush aside the shades of night,
In vibrant hues, proclaim the light.
For life anew, the canvas bold,
In resurrection's tale retold.

Resilience of the Heart

In shadows where the weary tread,
Faith whispers softly, a thread of light.
With each fall, the spirit is fed,
Rising strong, embracing the night.

The heart, a fortress, steadfast and bold,
Lessons learned from trials faced.
In every wound, a story unfolds,
Hope ignited, never erased.

In silence, prayers take wing and soar,
Yearning for solace, a guiding star.
With resilience, we knock on heaven's door,
Faith shall carry us near and far.

The dawn breaks, casting shadows away,
In the warmth of grace, we find our way.
Trust in the journey, come what may,
For love's embrace shall forever stay.

Through valleys deep, and mountains high,
Courage blooms like flowers in spring.
With open hearts, we aim for the sky,
In the dance of life, we rise and sing.

Labyrinth of Lost Faith

In the maze where questions intertwine,
Searching for echoes of truth's embrace.
Each turn a whisper, a waiting sign,
Yet shadows linger, a haunting trace.

With heavy hearts, we wander alone,
Seeking the light that flickers dim.
What was once vibrant now feels like stone,
Hope seems distant, the chance to brim.

But in the darkness, a spark persists,
A promise carved in the stone of time.
Amidst the tears, we clench our fists,
Courage arises, a mountain to climb.

In every loss, a lesson is found,
Like seeds of faith beneath the frost.
Through twisted paths, our souls are bound,
In struggle, our essence is not lost.

The labyrinth twists, but we will not break,
Our spirits dance through the storm's fierce ray.
With each step taken, the heart will awake,
Through faith reborn, we'll find our way.

Mosaic of the Fallen

In shards of glass, reflections gleam,
Echoes of beauty in broken form.
Each fragment tells a hidden dream,
In desolation, resilience is born.

A tapestry woven with trials and grace,
Every piece holds a story unique.
Through sorrowed paths, we find our place,
In unity's warmth, the spirit speaks.

Colors blend in a vibrant array,
Hues of struggle, wisdom's embrace.
Though fallen, we rise, come what may,
In the mosaic, we find our space.

With open hearts, we gather our pain,
Crafting beauty from what once was lost.
In the timeless dance of joy and rain,
The masterpiece shines, despite the cost.

As light breaks through each fractured hue,
We see the strength in what we hold dear.
The mosaic dances, forever new,
In love's embrace, we conquer our fear.

Consolation in Chaos

In the storm where tempests blow,
Peace is a whisper, a gentle sigh.
Through chaos' dance, we learn to grow,
In trust's soft cradle, we learn to fly.

With every trial, the heart expands,
Finding solace in the midnight gloom.
In tangled paths, destiny stands,
A light of hope breaks forth from doom.

As tumult roars, we seek the calm,
In the eye of storms, tranquility waits.
In faith's sweet song, we find the balm,
Healing hearts that love creates.

With courage as our steadfast guide,
We navigate the raging sea.
In chaos, grace will provide,
A gentle hand to set us free.

So let the winds of change arise,
For in each gust, we find our path.
Through trials faced, and starlit skies,
Consolation blooms in aftermath.

Echoes of Redemption

In the silence, whispers call,
Hearts awaken to the fall.
Grace abounds, lifting the shame,
In His love, we find our name.

Every tear, a story sung,
Finding peace where hope is strung.
Faith ignites, a burning flame,
In His truth, we aren't the same.

Chains of darkness start to break,
As we rise, the heavens shake.
Every burden cast aside,
In His arms, we bide our pride.

From the depths, our voices soar,
Through the trials, we implore.
Echoes of a love profound,
In His mercy, we are found.

Salvation's song, forever near,
In His presence, we have no fear.
With each breath, our spirits sing,
Hallelujah, our hearts take wing.

Scattered Prayers

In the morning mist, they rise,
Whispers drifting to the skies.
Hands uplifted, seeking grace,
Finding solace in His face.

Each request, a tender plea,
Bound by faith, we long to see.
Through the storms and darkest nights,
His love guides and shines the lights.

Broken hearts, no longer lost,
In our trials, we count the cost.
Hope restored, we lay them bare,
Every sorrow, a sacred prayer.

United in this sacred space,
Voices lifted, hearts embrace.
In the silence, answers gleam,
Faith can turn our tears to dream.

Moments shared, the spirit flows,
In each prayer, our love just grows.
Scattered prayers, a fragrant rise,
Bringing peace to weary sighs.

The Mosaic of Mercy

Fragments lost, now intertwined,
In His grace, our hearts aligned.
Colors bright, a vivid blend,
Each piece a story to transcend.

Through the cracks, the light pours in,
Healing wounds, erasing sin.
Every shard, a tale to tell,
In His arms, we all are well.

Moments stitched with love and care,
The broken made whole, laid bare.
In our weakness, strength takes hold,
In His mercy, pure and bold.

Together we form one design,
A beautiful path, divine.
In the imperfections, beauty glows,
In His love, our spirit grows.

From shattered dreams to vibrant hues,
In His light, we can't refuse.
The tapestry of life unfolds,
In His mercy, love beholds.

Gathered Remnants

From the ashes, we arise,
Bound by faith, we touch the skies.
Scattered souls in search of home,
In His arms, we learn to roam.

Every heart, a sacred thread,
Woven tightly, love we've fed.
As we gather, strength renews,
In His light, we chase the blues.

Fragments lost yet coming near,
In our voices, we hold dear.
Together now, we stand as one,
In His spirit, we have won.

Through the trials, we'll endure,
In His promise, we are sure.
Gathered remnants, hearts entwined,
In His grace, our hope aligned.

With each breath, we seek to know,
The endless love He aims to show.
Gathered in faith, we rise anew,
In His love, we'll always bloom.

Chalice of the Broken

In the quiet dusk, we gather near,
With hearts aflame and souls sincere.
The chalice raised, for all to see,
A symbol of grace, for you and me.

Fragments of dreams, like glass on stone,
Each piece a story, of love we've known.
Together we sip from this sacred cup,
With faith renewed, we lift it up.

In the shadows cast by sorrow's breath,
We find our strength even in death.
The wine of mercy flows like rain,
Healing the wounds, washing the pain.

O broken souls, lift up your plight,
In darkness, let us find the light.
For in our cracks, His love does shine,
A golden thread woven divine.

So raise the cup, let joy resound,
In shattered places, hope is found.
The chalice of the broken we share,
A testament of love, beyond compare.

Adoration Among the Ashes

Amidst the ruins, we kneel and pray,
In the hallowed ground, where spirits lay.
Ashes linger, a sacred sign,
To rise again, from dust divine.

Through the smoke, our voices soar,
In remembrance, we seek for more.
The songs of the lost, a whispering breeze,
Carried softly among the trees.

O heart, uplifted, in grief we stand,
Holding the memories, like grains of sand.
Each grain a moment, each moment a tear,
A testament to love that brought us here.

Among the ashes, we find our place,
In the warmth of the holy grace.
For in despair, a flicker ignites,
Turning the dark into radiant lights.

Let us gather, with reverence deep,
In sorrow's arms, our promises keep.
Adoration born from grief's embrace,
Turning the ashes to a sacred space.

Invocation for the Fractured

O shattered hearts, we call your name,
In the silence where sorrow came.
With open hands, we seek the One,
Who mends the fractures, His will be done.

From brokenness, a voice ascends,
A prayer that seeks to make amends.
In every fissure, His love shall flow,
Bringing forth healing, as rivers go.

O Lord of mercy, hear our plea,
In our disarray, we long to see.
The beauty hidden in shattered glass,
Reflecting light as shadows pass.

Invoke the strength in every tear,
For in our weakness, you draw near.
Hold us close in this tangled fight,
Transform our darkness into light.

From broken paths, we rise again,
With faith ignited, we shall sustain.
An invocation for all who fall,
In the grace of your love, we stand tall.

Shattered Altars

In the silence of the fallen stones,
We gather our hopes, our whispered tones.
The altars lie in fragments, bare,
Yet in their ruins, we find our prayer.

Each broken piece tells tales of old,
Of sacrifices made, of hearts bold.
Let us kneel where the cracks reveal,
The sacred truth that we can heal.

With trembling hands, we light a flame,
For every heart knows loss and pain.
In the ashes, new embers ignite,
Shattered altars, a beacon of light.

O faithful souls, come gather near,
In the intertwining of doubt and fear.
For from destruction, beauty grows,
In shattered altars, our spirit glows.

Let this place be a holy ground,
Where the hushed echoes of love abound.
In every fracture, a spark ignites,
Reviving the faith that conquers nights.

The Hopeful Parable of Longing

In the quiet whispers of the night,
Hearts lift to the stars so bright.
Yearning for a love divine,
In shadows, faith begins to shine.

The promise of dawn breaks the dark,
A flicker ignites every spark.
Longing is a sacred quest,
Finding peace within the unrest.

Through trials, the soul learns to see,
In absence, we find unity.
A tale of hope, woven tight,
In every tear, there blooms light.

The journey continues, hearts aligned,
With faith as the anchor, love refined.
Each step a prayer, each breath a song,
In the story of longing, we all belong.

So let us walk this path we share,
In silent grace and whispered prayer.
Hopeful hearts, forever strong,
In the hope of longing, we belong.

Transforming Tears into Testimony

When sorrow falls like gentle rain,
Each tear a testament of pain.
In the depths, the spirit bends,
Yet from the wound, a new life mends.

The heartache sings a solemn tune,
Beneath the weight, we find a rune.
Stories of struggle rise like steam,
From brokenness, we dare to dream.

In every sorrow, wisdom flows,
A river where true courage grows.
Each tear a seed of strength and grace,
In the dark night, a sacred place.

The trial is the forge of soul,
Transforming hurt, we find the whole.
From shadows, the light begins to gleam,
In testimony, we boldly beam.

Together we gather, hands entwined,
In shared stories, hearts aligned.
Turning tears into songs of might,
We rise anew, embracing the light.

Cinnamon and Ash: A Ritual of Renewal

Beneath the old oak, we gather round,
With cinnamon and ash on holy ground.
A ritual whispered in sacred tones,
As hearts are kindled, lost to stones.

Each sprinkle of spice, a prayer set free,
A dance of renewal, for you and me.
From ashes, we rise, reborn anew,
In the sacred circle, everything true.

The warmth of the spice, a touch of grace,
In solemn silence, we find our place.
The past is washed in the binding smoke,
In each breath spoken, a promise evoked.

In the stillness, a journey starts,
With every heartbeat, the spiritarts.
Cinnamon and ash, a fragrant blend,
In this renewal, we find the mend.

So here we stand, with hands held tight,
Embracing the blessings, welcoming light.
Through every cycle, the spirit flows,
In the ritual of life, true love grows.

Surrendering the Shattered

In the fragments of what we hold dear,
Lies the beauty cloaked in fear.
With every piece that falls away,
A new path beckons, come what may.

The broken heart sings a mournful song,
Yet through the cracks, the light grows strong.
Surrendering all that we cannot face,
Finding solace in divine grace.

The lessons learned in shattered dreams,
Bring forth a strength beyond our schemes.
With open hands, we let love in,
In surrender, we find where we begin.

With each shard lifted, our spirits soar,
What once divided now binds us more.
Through brokenness, the truth is clear,
In surrendering, we conquer fear.

So let us lay our burdens down,
In the ashes, we wear a crown.
For through surrender, we unveil the art,
Of living with an open heart.

Divine Restoration

Through shadows deep, a light will find,
The weary soul, the heart entwined.
With grace that mends the fractured clay,
In every struggle, hope will stay.

In whispers soft, the spirit heals,
A promise made, the heart reveals.
From ashes born, the beauty grows,
In faith revived, our spirit glows.

The burdens lifted, chains undone,
With every dawn, a new begun.
In sacred acts, our strength restored,
In love embraced, we are adored.

Transformation flows, like river wide,
In faith we walk, with God as guide.
The wounds of time, with mercy blend,
In unity, our souls transcend.

So let us rise on wings of grace,
In every trial, we find our place.
With open hearts, we journey forth,
In divine love, we find our worth.

The Light in the Cracks

Beneath the weight of solemn night,
There shines a spark, a gentle light.
In broken places, hope ignites,
A flicker bold that love unites.

Through shattered dreams and strife we face,
The tender touch of endless grace.
In every flaw, a story turns,
In deepest wounds, true beauty burns.

The cracks of life, where shadows dwell,
Hold sacred truths, our spirits swell.
From gaps of pain, we bravely grow,
In tender hands, God's love will show.

Reflections sweet of joy and sorrow,
In whispered prayers, we find tomorrow.
So may we see with open eyes,
The light that shines, our hearts' reprise.

We gather pieces, small and dear,
A tapestry of hope draws near.
In every struggle, grace prevails,
With faith in hand, our spirit sails.

Salvaging Sacred Moments

In quiet corners, time stands still,
In fleeting breath, our hearts fulfill.
Each sacred pause, a treasure found,
In stillness speaks the joy profound.

The moments lost, we seek to save,
In every laugh, in every wave.
Amidst the rush, God's hand we feel,
In tender whispers, our hearts heal.

A sunset's glow, a child's first laugh,
In simple things, we find our path.
In memories woven, the soul expands,
In gentle touch, the Spirit stands.

We gather sparks, like stars above,
In shared embrace, we find our love.
Through shared stories, grace we share,
In every trial, God's presence there.

Let's cherish moments, pure and bright,
For in these gifts, we find the light.
With thankful hearts, we greet each dawn,
In sacred time, we live as one.

The Whisper of Renewal

In every dawn, a promise sings,
The softest breath, a new hope brings.
In nature's song, the spirit wakes,
In quietude, the heart remakes.

The weary wanderer finds a way,
In gentle whispers, night meets day.
The cycle turns, as seasons flow,
In every end, new beginnings grow.

From barren ground, the flowers rise,
In tender light, the heart complies.
With every leaf that falls in grace,
We witness truth in time's embrace.

A spirit rich, rejuvenates,
In every breath, the heart awaits.
Through trials faced and storms we brave,
In love and faith, we find the wave.

So let us stand, renewed and bold,
In whispered prayers, our truth unfolds.
In every heart, a sacred spark,
Together we ignite the dark.

Songs of the Assembled

In the silence of prayer, hearts unite,
Voices rise up to the radiant light.
Each soul a note in harmonious grace,
Together we journey in this sacred space.

Hands uplifted, we seek to belong,
In the warmth of the faithful, we grow strong.
Chanting our hopes, in rhythm divine,
A symphony born from the love we find.

Through trials and shadows, we hold the flame,
Seeking the path that upholds His name.
With faith as our anchor, we stand as one,
In the dance of the Spirit, our fears are undone.

Beneath the stars, our prayers take flight,
In the depth of the night, we seek His light.
Each breath a promise, a vow we renew,
In the whispers of grace, His presence rings true.

Together we rise, like the dawn of the day,
With every heartbeat, we find our way.
In the songs of the gathered, our voices ascend,
In the harmony of love, our spirits mend.

Each Tear a Testament

In the valley of sorrows, our hearts feel the weight,
Each tear is a story, each cry a fate.
We gather our pain, like rain in the night,
A testament written in trials' harsh light.

Through the darkness we wander, yet hope shines still,
With every teardrop, a whisper of will.
Each pain shared is a burden made light,
In the healing embrace of compassion's pure sight.

For in every sorrow, the spirit does grow,
A seed of resilience, nurtured in woe.
With faith as our guide, we rise from the deep,
Finding strength in the shadows, in promises we keep.

As we gather our tears, like pearls on a string,
Each moment a blessing, each heart a new spring.
United in struggle, we honor the way,
In the tapestry woven, our truths will convey.

So let the tears flow, a river of grace,
Each drop an offering, a sacred embrace.
Together we stand, through joy and through pain,
In the book of our lives, love's message will reign.

Transcending the Shattered

In the cracks of our hearts, the light finds a way,
Transforming our hurt into dawn's soft array.
With each broken shard, a new vision we see,
Rising from fragments, our spirits set free.

Through trials that test us, we uncover the gold,
In the ashes of doubt, a story unfolds.
In the midst of the chaos, we seek the unseen,
Finding strength in the struggle, the layers between.

Hope dances lightly on paths paved with pain,
In the remnants of sorrow, new life shall remain.
We gather the pieces, each loss a rebirth,
In the beauty of healing, we find our true worth.

With courage, we walk through the valleys of strife,
Embracing each moment, the struggle of life.
Transcending the shattered, our spirits ascend,
In unity forged, we learn to depend.

So let us remember, in darkness, there's grace,
In every broken heart, a unique sacred space.
Together we flourish, through trials we grow,
In the light of our love, we're never alone.

The Beauty of the Broken

In the remnants of pain, there shines a great truth,
The beauty of broken is rooted in youth.
From scars we arise, embracing our flaws,
In the tapestry woven, we find worthy cause.

Through struggles we learn, our hearts gently mend,
In vulnerability's light, we discover a friend.
Each crack a reminder, each blemish a gift,
In the hands of the Maker, our spirits uplift.

May we honor our journeys, with all that we bear,
For within every fracture, love shows us care.
In the softest of whispers we hear heaven's song,
Revealing the truth that we all must belong.

So let us embrace all, our stories untold,
For in the beauty of broken, our lives unfold.
In shared imperfections, we stand side by side,
With each wounded heart, we can trust and abide.

Through the trials of life, let us always see,
The beauty of broken illuminates free.
Together we flourish, imperfect yet strong,
In the art of our lives, we are all part of the song.

Salvaging the Sacred

In the hush of the twilight hour,
We seek the light, the guiding power.
With faith as our compass, we walk the path,
Embracing love, shunning wrath.

Through trials of fire, we rise anew,
Cleansed by tears, our spirits true.
The discarded whisper, a sacred call,
In unity's grace, we stand tall.

The past may dim, yet hope ignites,
Each flicker leads to divine heights.
In hands outstretched, we reclaim our dreams,
For within the heart, the sacred redeems.

In echoes of prayer, our voices blend,
In the tapestry of life, we mend.
The sacred threads, woven tight,
Guide us home through darkest night.

With every heartbeat, we sing a song,
Of salvation's journey, where we belong.
Together in spirit, never apart,
Salvaging the sacred, with open heart.

Whispers of Redemption

In shadows deep, the whispers rise,
Carried on winds, beyond the skies.
Each word a promise, woven with care,
Redemption beckons, in silent prayer.

Beneath the weight of burdens worn,
New hopes awaken, from sorrows born.
With every tear, a river flows,
Through valleys of doubt, the spirit grows.

The soul ignites, like summer's blaze,
In shadows' grip, we find our ways.
With gentle hands, grace weaves its art,
Whispers of love, to heal the heart.

In the stillness, truth breaks through,
A tapestry rich in every hue.
From ashes rise, we take our stand,
Redemption's call, a guiding hand.

In the light of dawn, new visions bloom,
Cleansed by faith, dispelling gloom.
With every step, we write our tale,
Whispers of redemption, we shall prevail.

Ashes to Altar

From the remnants of pain, we build anew,
Out of despair, faith breaks through.
In the quiet, where shadows fade,
Ashes to altar, in love we're remade.

The past now speaks in muted tones,
Each memory carved in heart of stone.
With grace, we gather what seems lost,
To honor the journey, embrace the cost.

In every ember, a promise shines,
The sacred dance of intertwining lines.
With hearts ignited, we rise as one,
From ashes we rise, our fears outrun.

On altars built with hope and tears,
We forge a path, amid our fears.
In silent reverence, we bow and pray,
Transforming ashes to light each day.

In the glow of love, our spirits soar,
From devastation, we find the door.
With every breath, we chant the song,
Ashes to altar, where we belong.

The Resurrection of Reflection

In stillness found, the mirror gleams,
Reflecting truth, unveiling dreams.
In shadows past, we find the grace,
The resurrection of each face.

With hearts awakened, we softly plea,
For wisdom's light, to set us free.
Through trials faced, we gather strength,
In every step, we traverse length.

The journey long, but worth the fight,
In darkness found, we seek the light.
With every whisper, a world reborn,
Reflection brings hope, where hearts have worn.

From ashes of doubt, to faith anew,
In brokenness, we find the true.
With eyes raised high, we greet the dawn,
The resurrection of our spirit's song.

In moments sacred, we learn to see,
The tapestry woven, you and me.
Together we rise, beyond the fear,
In reflection we find, our path is clear.

Lifting Broken Spirits

In shadows we dwell, seeking the light,
A whisper of grace in the depth of the night.
He gathers our sorrows, our burdens He'll share,
With love everlasting, beyond all compare.

Through valleys of anguish, He walks by our side,
A beacon of hope, our fear He'll abide.
With hands outstretched wide, He lifts us anew,
In the warmth of His embrace, we're born to pursue.

In prayers soft murmur, His presence we feel,
A balm for the spirit, His touch can heal.
Each tear that we shed, He holds in His hand,
Transforming our pain, with a love so grand.

So let us rise up, our hearts intertwined,
In faith we shall flourish, in hope we'll find.
With every new dawn, may our spirits enchance,
In lifting each other, we find our true chance.

Fragrant Offerings

In quiet devotion, we gather as one,
With hearts opened wide, and faith like the sun.
Each prayer a petal, each song a sweet praise,
A fragrant offering that never decays.

Through rituals sacred and gestures of love,
We uplift our spirits to God up above.
With each whispered prayer, our souls intertwine,
In the warmth of His presence, we know we are divine.

With incense as prayer, we rise through the air,
A symbol of hope, of joy and of care.
May our lives be a garden, forever to bloom,
As we share in His light, dispelling all gloom.

In gratitude's depth, we lay our hearts bare,
With fervent thanksgiving, our burdens we share.
Each moment a blessing, each step a delight,
In fragrant offerings, we find our true sight.

The Tapestry of Hope

In the weave of our lives, threads intertwine,
Each joy and each sorrow, a design so divine.
With colors of faith, we stitch day by day,
Embroidering love in a luminous way.

Through trials and triumphs, our spirits endure,
In the depths of despair, our hearts remain pure.
With every new stitch, He guides us with grace,
Creating a story that time can't erase.

In the tapestry vibrant, each soul plays a part,
A picture of hope woven deep in the heart.
In fellowship's cradle, we find our embrace,
Together in unity, we seek His face.

So let us be mindful of every thread bright,
For together we flourish in love's sacred light.
With hands held together, our spirits shall rise,
In the tapestry of hope, we'll reach for the skies.

From Ruins to Revival

Amidst the decay, a whisper ignites,
From ashes and rubble, new hope takes flight.
With faith as our compass, we rise from the dust,
Rebuilding our lives, in His wisdom we trust.

With every broken heart, He fashions anew,
Restoring our strength, making old things break through.
From shadows of doubt, a brilliance shall gleam,
In the arms of our Savior, we find our true dream.

In gardens of sorrow, new blossoms will bloom,
Transforming the night, dispelling the gloom.
With courage Divine, we'll walk through each trial,
From ruins to revival, we journey in style.

As phoenixes rise, from fires and pain,
With hearts intertwined, our love will remain.
In unity forged, we shall flourish and thrive,
In faith we emerge, from ruins to revival.

The Divine Art of Arranging

In the silence of prayer, we find a way,
Each note of our hearts, in chorus, will sway.
A tapestry woven in love divine,
Guiding our spirits, with hope we align.

The brush of the heavens paints paths of grace,
In every soul's journey, His light we embrace.
With each gentle whisper, the cosmos sings,
To the rhythm of mercy, the joy that it brings.

In moments of chaos, His wisdom appears,
A dance of the ages, transcending our fears.
The stars as our witness, the moon's tender glow,
In the divine art, His presence we know.

From the depths of our trials, a beauty is born,
Through shadows, we rise, unbroken, reborn.
Each step in His world, a step towards light,
In the grand tapestry, we shine ever bright.

As we gather our hopes, and sow love anew,
In the fields of eternity, He's tender and true.
With gratitude flowing, our spirits ascend,
In the divine art of life, we find our true friend.

Harmony from Dissonance

From discordant whispers, a melody grows,
In the heart of compassion, a symphony flows.
With every lost note, a new song begins,
Resilience and love, the harmony wins.

Through valleys of shadows, where darkness does creep,
A flicker of faith, in whispers, we keep.
The clash of our burdens, the trials we bear,
Transform into beauty, with strength born of prayer.

In the storm's wild embrace, we seek the calm sound,
With every step forward, new purpose is found.
Together as one, we rise and unite,
In the tapestry woven, our souls are alight.

The echoes of sorrow are woven to grace,
Each tear that we shed, a holy embrace.
From each fracture of pain, a new truth will gleam,
In the heart of the struggle, we find our true dream.

In harmony's cradle, we dance through the strife,
With love as our beacon, the song of our life.
Through dissonance tangled, we find our true voice,
In the music of grace, together rejoice.

Scraps of the Sacred

In the fragments of moments, the divine concealed,
A whisper of truth, in chaos revealed.
The path may be rocky, yet beauty is near,
In the scraps of the sacred, our spirits draw near.

Like petals of faith scattered wide by the breeze,
Each piece tells a story, to comfort, to please.
In the tapestry woven with threads made of light,
The smallest of fragments spark hope in the night.

From ashes of strife, new life will emerge,
In the quiet of prayer, our souls will converge.
A gathering of pieces, each one plays a role,
In the dance of the sacred, we heal and console.

In laughter and sorrow, the sacred we find,
In the spaces between, our hearts are aligned.
With every lost moment, grace lingers and stays,
In the scraps of the sacred, love lights up our ways.

As we cherish these fragments, we come to behold,
The beauty of life, in each story told.
In the quiet of evening, as daylight departs,
The scraps of the sacred, forever in our hearts.

Light Through the Cracks

In the walls of our being, where shadows reside,
The light breaks through cracks, the darkness can't hide.
With every soft glow, there's hope to be found,
In the refuge of love, our spirits are crowned.

With courage we gather the shards of our heart,
In the dance of the broken, a brand new art.
For where there is struggle, and battles are fought,
The light shines the brightest, on lessons we sought.

In the echo of sorrow, a warmth will unfold,
As the dawn of forgiveness begins to take hold.
With each fragile beam, a promise unfolds,
In the cracks of our souls, love's beauty beholds.

Through valleys and mountains, we journey as one,
In the tapestry woven, our spirit is spun.
Every fracture a blessing, each wound a new phase,
In light through the cracks, we discover new ways.

As we embrace all the parts, both broken and whole,
In the light that breaks through, we find our true role.
With faith as our guide, we'll dance through the night,
For the cracks in our hearts let the heavens ignite.

Born Again in Splendor

In shadows deep, the light awakes,
A heart renewed, the old one shakes.
With whispers soft, grace does arrive,
In holy love, the soul will thrive.

From ashes pure, a fire ignites,
In humbled prayer, we seek the heights.
A phoenix rise, in faith's embrace,
Born again, we seek His face.

In sacred waters, we are washed,
A promise kept, redemption's cost.
In every tear, a lesson learned,
From darkness bright, the candle burned.

Through trials fierce, the spirit grows,
In every storm, His mercy flows.
With gratitude, our voices sing,
In harmony, our praises ring.

In every heart, His love will dwell,
In faith we stand, our stories tell.
From doubt to trust, in Him we stand,
Forever bound, in His great hand.

Branches from the Ruins

From broken ground, new life shall bloom,
In barren lands, dispelling gloom.
With leaves of hope, we stretch and sway,
In faith we find the light of day.

Though storms may rage, and roots may ache,
We hold our ground, for love's own sake.
Each branch that grows, a tale to share,
Of strength in spirit, everywhere.

In every wound, the healing starts,
In unity, we mend our hearts.
With prayerful hands, we cultivate,
A forest strong, where dreams await.

As shadows fade, the sun breaks through,
In sacred silence, life feels new.
We reach for sky, our spirits raise,
In gratitude, we sing His praise.

From ruins high, our roots expand,
In trust we stand, a faithful band.
With branches wide, we shelter all,
In loving grace, we rise, we call.

Stained Glass Reflections

In colored light, our spirits dance,
Each shard a story, a sacred chance.
The windows speak of love divine,
In every hue, a heart's design.

When sunlight streams through artful panes,
A symphony of joy remains.
The past and present intertwine,
In vibrant ways, His love will shine.

With gentle hands, they craft the frame,
To hold the light, to speak His name.
As shadows blend and colors merge,
Our souls awake, in faith we surge.

Through every break, the beauty sings,
In every heart, redemption clings.
Together we, a work of art,
In stained glass dreams, we play our part.

In quiet moments, reflections flow,
The light within begins to grow.
Through every piece, in love we'll see,
A tapestry of unity.

The Echo of Solace

In gentle whispers, His voice we hear,
Through every doubt, dispelling fear.
With every heartbeat, He draws us near,
In silence deep, our path is clear.

The echo calls, a guiding light,
In darkest nights, He shines so bright.
A balm for wounds, a soothing balm,
In troubled times, we find our calm.

With every prayer, the spirit flows,
In sacred trust, our love still grows.
The peace within, a precious gift,
In grace we stand, our hearts uplift.

Through every tear, the solace stays,
In heartfelt songs, our voices raise.
From depths of sorrow, we rise again,
In unity, as family, friends.

So hear the echo, soft and clear,
In every moment, He draws near.
With faith ablaze, we journey on,
In love's embrace, forever strong.

Fragments of Faith

In shadows deep, we seek the light,
A guiding hand, dispelling night.
With whispered prayers our hearts ascend,
On fragile wings, to You we tend.

In trials faced, our spirits rise,
Through storms of doubt, we claim the skies.
Each broken piece, a testament,
To love bestowed, to lives well-sent.

Your promise echoes, ever true,
In every heart, the hope anew.
Through faith we stand, though fears may wane,
Together bound, our souls sustain.

In quiet moments, we reflect,
On paths paved bright, Your love perfect.
With every heartbeat, we find grace,
In fragments whole, our sacred space.

So let us rise, unite our prayer,
In harmony, we shall declare.
For in our hearts, Your light will shine,
Fragments of faith, forever thine.

Threads of Grace

In tapestry of lives entwined,
A thread of grace in love defined.
With every stitch, a story shared,
In faith and hope, our hearts laid bare.

Woven gently, through joy and strife,
The vibrant hues enhance our life.
Each knot a blessing, lessons learned,
In every twist, the heart's discerned.

From darkened days to radiant skies,
Your presence walks where turning lies.
Through trials faced, we find our strength,
In threads of grace, we span the lengths.

So let us hold, our fabric tight,
In woven bonds, we find the light.
Together strong, not lost, but found,
In threads of grace, true love unbound.

With every dawn, new colors gleam,
In sacred fabric, we can dream.
For in this weave, we are embraced,
In every heart, Your love is traced.

Healing from Ashes

From ashes cold, a spark ignites,
In brokenness, the spirit fights.
Each ember holds a whispered prayer,
For healing grace, we find You there.

In silent night, our pains laid bare,
With trust, we seek the sweet repair.
Through trials faced, we learn to rise,
With faith anew, we touch the skies.

In every tear, a lesson found,
In ashes gray, hope's voice resounds.
Through darkest paths, Your light will gleam,
To heal our hearts, fulfill the dream.

In tender grace, we mend the fray,
A journey forged, come what may.
From ashes fall, to wings we soar,
For through the pain, we seek You more.

So let us trust, in love's embrace,
For from the dust, we see Your face.
With every breath, we rise anew,
Healing from ashes, guided by You.

Rebuilding the Sanctuary

In quiet realms, we seek the space,
To build anew, our sacred place.
With prayers uplifted, hands combine,
In unity, Your will align.

Through every crack, Your light comes through,
In broken walls, a vision true.
We gather strength, both young and old,
In love's embrace, our hearts unfold.

From rubble vast, we raise the beam,
A home restored, a faithful dream.
Each stone a story, every heart,
In this great work, we each take part.

With faith as our foundation strong,
The melody of love's sweet song.
As weary souls, we find our rest,
In sanctuary built to bless.

So let us rise, our spirits soar,
Rebuilding lives, to love and more.
For in this work, we find our way,
In sanctuary, forever stay.

A Garden from the Grief

In sorrow's soil, we plant our seeds,
With tears like rain, our spirit bleeds.
Yet from the dark, a bloom shall rise,
In humble faith beneath the skies.

Each petal holds a prayer's embrace,
Reflecting love, a sacred space.
For in the pain, comes beauty's hand,
A garden flourishes as we stand.

The roots entwined, through loss we grow,
In every heart, a light we sow.
Though storms may come, and shadows creep,
In faith's own arms, we find our keep.

Let grief transform to hope's bright hue,
As dawn reveals the morning dew.
For in the quiet, whispers share,
A garden blooms with love and care.

The Promise of Solar Flare

From darkness deep, a light descends,
A promise born where every heart mends.
The solar flare ignites the skies,
A blazing truth that never dies.

In golden rays, we see His grace,
Each moment held in time and space.
A warmth that warms our weary souls,
In faith's embrace, our spirit strolls.

As shadows flee, the dawn breaks clear,
Resurrection whispers in our ear.
With every pulse, the universe sings,
A testament to the love He brings.

In cosmic dance, creation swells,
The promise held in sacred spells.
Through trials we find the strength to share,
Our souls ignited by a solar flare.

Traced in Divine Dust

In the quiet corners of the earth,
We seek the mark of sacred birth.
With every step, the dust we tread,
Is laced with dreams and prayers unsaid.

Each grain a story, each path a song,
In divine dust, we all belong.
Tracing lines of lives entwined,
A tapestry of love defined.

In valleys low, and mountains high,
We find our purpose, never shy.
Hand in hand, through time we roam,
For every heart can find its home.

Let faith's embrace lead us anew,
In the dust, God's vision true.
For in our journey, grace we trust,
We walk the world, traced in divine dust.

The Lament of the Redeemed

In shadows cast, our voices rise,
A lament sweet, beneath the skies.
For what was lost, the heart does mourn,
Through pain's embrace, our souls reborn.

Forgiven past, our burdens weigh,
Yet hope shines bright, a guiding ray.
Each tear a testament of grace,
In love's embrace, we find our place.

Through trials faced, we gather near,
In every loss, a truth so clear.
The path of light through darkest night,
In faith's own arms, we find our fight.

With voices raised, we sing our hymn,
The wounds may close, yet love won't dim.
In every heartbeat, love's refrain,
The lament speaks of joy through pain.

Threads of Divinity Woven

In the loom of life, each thread we share,
Ties us to the heavens, a bond so rare.
Woven with love, in colors so bright,
Guided by the stars, in the quiet night.

With hands of grace, the fabric unfolds,
Whispers of hope in the stories it holds.
Each stitch a prayer, each knot a vow,
Weaving our faith in the here and now.

Across the ages, the tapestry grows,
In every challenge, divinity flows.
A sacred design, both fragile and strong,
Binding our spirits, where we all belong.

In moments of doubt, let the fibers unite,
For in every shadow, there shines a light.
Through trials we face, let love be the thread,
For the heart of the world is where we are led.

Threads of divinity, gentle and bold,
In the fabric of life, our story unfolds.
Together we stand, in joy and in pain,
Woven in grace, like sunshine and rain.

Reverence in Ruins

In the silence of decay, echoes remain,
Whispers of worship amidst the pain.
Among the fallen, a spirit ignites,
Reviving the hope in the darkest nights.

Cracked stones and shadows hold stories untold,
A testament to faith that never grows old.
In reverence we gather, as dust meets the skies,
Finding sanctuary where ancient hope lies.

Through the remnants of life, we seek the divine,
In brokenness find how our souls intertwine.
The ruins teach wisdom, the heart learns to bend,
In the ashes of sorrow, new beginnings extend.

With every step taken on paths lined with grief,
We embrace the sacred, and find our relief.
In mourning we rise, our spirits attest,
That reverence blooms in the ruins we bless.

So let us honor the places we tread,
Where the light meets the dark, and the living are wed.
In the heart of decay, we unearth the truth,
Reverence in ruins, eternal and soothed.

Healing the Fractured Spirit

In the stillness of prayer, the heart starts to mend,
Whispers of solace like a balm we send.
Each breath a reminder of love's gentle grace,
Healing the spirit, embracing the space.

The wounds that we carry, carved deep in our souls,
Yearn for the light that the spirit consoles.
In unity, let us gather and bind,
The pieces of hope that we've struggled to find.

Through trials and sorrows, the lessons unfold,
In the warmth of forgiveness, our stories are told.
With patience we nurture the fragile within,
In the garden of grace, new life shall begin.

As tears wash the earth, the heart learns to soar,
In the embrace of compassion, we open the door.
With every kind gesture, our spirits unite,
Healing the fractured, transforming the night.

So let us walk gently on paths made of light,
With faith as our guide through the shadowed plight.
For in every connection, our spirits are free,
Healing the fractures, together we'll be.

Sacred Reconstruction

In the rubble of dreams, we gather the parts,
With faith as our blueprint, we mend broken hearts.
From ashes of loss, a vision takes flight,
Sacred reconstruction, reclaims the light.

Each fragment a lesson, each scar a new page,
In the story of life, we find our true sage.
With hands intertwined, we build with great care,
A sanctuary born in the depths of our prayer.

Through trials we navigate, together we stand,
Crafting a future, united, and grand.
The spirit of love, in our structures erect,
Guiding each hammer, each nail we connect.

Through the whispers of hope, our hearts resonate,
For in every foundation, new dreams cultivate.
In the strength of our bond, we find wisdom's call,
Sacred reconstruction, uplifting us all.

Let us honor the journey, the cracks that we show,
For in every challenge, love continues to grow.
With faith as our mortar, we rise and transform,
In sacred reconstruction, our spirits are warm.

Pieces of a Divine Puzzle

In the tapestry of grace we weave,
Each thread a story, each knot a belief.
A sovereign hand guides the stray,
Bringing light to the shadows of the day.

Mountains of hope rise bold in our hearts,
Whispers of faith play their sacred parts.
In fractures and gaps, His love does shine,
Revealing the beauty of a design divine.

Every tear a glimmer, a gem of His love,
Transformation unfolds in the skies above.
We gather the pieces, though some may be lost,
He leads us with mercy, no matter the cost.

Fragments of longing, our souls do hold,
In the arms of the Father, our stories are told.
Aligning the broken with threads of pure light,
We find in each struggle a path to the right.

In the dance of creation, we hear the call,
A symphony sacred that unites us all.
For in every puzzle, the truth shall ignite,
A masterpiece forged in the darkest of night.

Mending the Heart's Canvas

In whispers of silence, the painter draws near,
With colors of hope that dissolve every fear.
The canvas of sorrow, He tenderly tends,
With strokes of compassion, the heart slowly mends.

Each brush a reminder of grace unconfined,
In strokes of forgiveness, our spirits aligned.
For wounds of the past are mere shadows now,
As the artist's light bids the broken to bow.

The palette of life, with its vibrant hues,
Speaks of redemption in the loving muse.
Layer upon layer, the truth is displayed,
The beauty of healing in His love conveyed.

In the depths of despair, a vision is framed,
With shades of resilience that cannot be tamed.
The heart's canvas glows, a miraculous sight,
Transformed through the darkness, embraced by the light.

So let us be vessels, our art to unfold,
Each story a blessing, each struggle, pure gold.
For mending the heart is a sacred decree,
In the gallery of faith, we are finally free.

Salvaged Sanctuary

In the ruins of anguish, a solace is found,
A sanctuary built on the hallowed ground.
With every broken stone, a prayer is laid,
A refuge of faith where shadows do fade.

Amidst the debris, the light filters through,
Whispers of safety in hopes born anew.
Each captured moment, a memory's embrace,
We gather our fragments, our fears we replace.

The walls stand tall, a testament true,
To love that endures and makes whole what is due.
Resilient and caring, the heart does extend,
In salvaged sanctuary, all wounds find their mend.

Beneath the arches, a chorus does rise,
In stories of healing, we find the skies.
We are all pilgrims, seeking to learn,
In the ashes of pain, there's always a turn.

For every sanctuary, a tale must be told,
Of solace discovered in places of old.
Together we stand, with spirits set free,
In the salvaged embrace of our sacred decree.

Pilgrimage Through Turmoil

On paths of confusion where silence does reign,
Each step is a struggle, each moment, a strain.
But through every stumble, a lesson we gain,
In the pilgrimage onward, our faith will sustain.

Through valleys of shadows, we search for the light,
With courage ignited, we face the long night.
The journey is winding, yet firmly we tread,
Bound by the promise that nourishes dread.

With each breath, the whispers of comfort resound,
In the depths of torment, our spirits are found.
For through every trial, we seek what is true,
In the dance of the storm, He will see us through.

It's here in the struggle, the clarity blooms,
In the chaos of life, our destiny looms.
So take heart, dear traveler, you're never alone,
In the pilgrimage onward, His love is your own.

By faith we are guided, by hope we will stride,
Through turmoil and trials, we carry His light.
For each step forward is a step toward grace,
And in unity's arms, we shall find our place.

Seraphim Among the Ruins

Upon the stones where shadows creep,
The Seraphim in silence weep.
Wings of light, in softer gloom,
Guide lost souls through ancient tombs.

Echoes of a broken choir,
Lift their voices, never tire.
In the ruins, grace will bloom,
Awakening from endless gloom.

Among the dust, their presence glows,
Invisible, yet love bestows.
Carved in faith, they stand so tall,
Guardians of the earth's great fall.

Whispers of the lost, they hear,
Filling hearts with holy cheer.
In each crack where shadows lie,
Seraphim lift souls to the sky.

So rise, dear heart, from ashes gray,
The Seraphim shall light your way.
With every breath, let hope expand,
For in the ruins, they shall stand.

The Lament of Rebirth

In the stillness of the night,
A whisper calls to hearts in plight.
Born of sorrow, yet so bright,
The lament sings of future light.

Tears fall gently, like the rain,
Washing clean the wounds of pain.
In each sigh, there lies a way,
To rise anew with each new day.

From ashes cold, the phoenix flies,
A dance of hope beneath the skies.
And in the dark, a voice will say,
'From death to life, we find our way.'

Fragile dreams begin to mend,
As nature's hand begins to tend.
In the pause, where grief once flowed,
A seed of faith begins to grow.

So let the loss not be in vain,
For every heart shall love again.
In every end, a brand new start,
The lament echoes in the heart.

Beyond the Shattered Threshold

At the threshold, where shadows fade,
Hope emerges, unafraid.
Beyond the dark, the light will break,
A promise kept, a vow we make.

Through shattered glass and twisted dreams,
Truth slips in through silent seams.
Each step is fraught with doubt and fear,
Yet faith will guide, and love draw near.

In broken paths, we find our way,
With every tear that falls today.
For in the ruin of what we've known,
New life will flourish, seeds be sown.

So stand, dear heart, and take your breath,
Embrace the journey, dance with death.
Beyond the door, there lies the chance,
To leap with faith, to dream, to dance.

For every break can forge a bond,
In shattered spaces, we respond.
Beyond the threshold, souls will soar,
A radiant spark forevermore.

Graceful Embrace of Defiance

In the shadow of despair,
There blooms a flower, rare and fair.
With petals soft and colors bold,
The grace of defiance, a story told.

Waves of doubt may crash and roar,
Yet love will rise and seek for more.
With every trial, we grow strong,
In our defiance, we belong.

The world may push, yet we stand tall,
In unity, we rise and call.
Our spirits entwined, deeply bound,
In the embrace of hope, we're found.

So let the storm come, fierce and wild,
For in our hearts, we are the child.
When faced with darkness, we will shine,
In every struggle, grace defines.

Stand firm, dear soul, against the flame,
In the embrace, we'll rise the same.
With love ablaze, fierce and free,
Defiance in grace, our destiny.